Baseball's MVPs

READING POWER

RYAN HOWARD

Joe Gaspar

PowerKiDS press
New York

Published in 2011 by The Rosen Publishing Group, Inc.
29 East 21st Street, New York, NY 10010

First Edition

Editor: Amelie von Zumbusch
Book Design: Kate Laczynski
Photo Researcher: Jessica Gerweck

Photo Credits: Cover, p. 1 Rob Leiter/Getty Images; pp. 4–5 Nick Laham/Getty Images; pp. 6–7, 10–11, 20 Rich Pilling/MLB photos via Getty Images; pp. 8–9 Mitchell Layton/MLB photos via Getty Images; pp. 12–13, 18–19 John Capella/Sports Imagery/Getty Images; pp. 14–15 Drew Hallowell/Getty Images Sport/Getty Images; pp. 16–17 Chris McGrath/Getty Images; p. 22 Elsa/Getty Images.

Library of Congress Cataloging-in-Publication Data

Gaspar, Joe.
Ryan Howard / Joe Gaspar.
p. cm. — (Baseball's mvps)
Includes index.
ISBN 978-1-4488-0632-4 (library binding) —
ISBN 978-1-4488-1788-7 (pbk.) — ISBN 978-1-4488-1789-4 (6-pack)
1. Howard, Ryan, 1979—Juvenile literature. 2. Baseball players—United States—Biography—Juvenile literature. I. Title.
GV865.H67G37 2011
796.357092—dc22
[B]

2009054257

Manufactured in the United States of America

CPSIA Compliance Information: Batch #WS10PK: For Further Information contact Rosen Publishing, New York, New York at 1-800-237-9932

CONTENTS

HK

Ryan Howard is a
baseball player.
He plays for the
Philadelphia Phillies.

Howard is a great player. He plays first base.

Rawlings
Authentic
Majestic

Howard was born in Saint Louis, Missouri. He grew up there, too.

Ryan Howard **bats** left-handed.

HOWARD
6

Howard is a great hitter. He hits many home runs.

In 2005, Howard played his first full year with the Phillies.

HOWARD
6

Howard gets along well with his teammates. He is a team leader.

In 2006, Howard was named the MVP, or most **valuable** player, in the National **League**.

Phillies

Authentic
COLLECTION
08

The Phillies won the **World Series** in 2008. Howard was happy and proud!

Howard loves baseball. He is one of the country's top players.

BOOKS

Here are more books to read about Ryan Howard and baseball:

Rasemas, Joe and Pat Sherman. *What It's Like to Be Ryan Howard / Qué se siente al ser Ryan Howard*. Hockessin, DE: Mitchell Lane Publishers, Inc., 2010.

Savage, Jeff. *Ryan Howard*. Amazing Athletes. Minneapolis, MN: First Avenue Editions, 2008.

WEB SITES

Due to the changing nature of Internet links, PowerKids Press has developed an online list of Web sites related to the subject of this book. This site is updated regularly. Please use this link to access the list:
www.powerkidslinks.com/bmvp/rh/

GLOSSARY

bats (BATS) Takes a turn trying to hit a baseball.

league (LEEG) A group of sports teams.

valuable (VAL-yoo-bul) Important.

World Series (WURLD SEER-eez) A group of games in which the two best baseball teams play against each other.

INDEX